KNOWING
AND
BELIEVING
THE LOVE OF
GOD
DEVOTIONAL

KURT OWEN

Edited by Shaun W. Smith & Amy Krachenfels

Publisher's Note:

ISBN 978-1-64970-403-0

9 781649 704030 >

www.KurtOwen.com

Cover design, Internal formatting & layout by: Hemant Lal
www.AaronProductionsIndia.com

ACKNOWLEDGEMENTS

I am very grateful for the help of Liz Alonge, Gene Harris, and Shaun Smith in editing this set of devotionals.

Shaun was also instrumental in the overall creation of it as was Michael and Jan Zoyes for which I am also grateful. They successfully spearheaded projects that almost made it so I HAD TO write this material.

I would also like to thank Pastor Sydney Ropp who cared enough about me to make sure I was understood even when I did not care.

Without Amy Krachenfels this book nor many others would not have been possible. For all of you who like my books, Amy is the person to whom you should be grateful. I am also very grateful for Amy's heart toward The Lord and Terry and me.

Speaking of Terry, my dad Jim Andrews introduced me to God's love in human form, but Terry made it a revelation. Without her, I am not sure I would have ever known true love personally. Forever am I grateful to her. Forever am I in love with her.

First and Last of it all, as cliche, as it sounds, I must thank God my Father and my Lord Jesus. Without them being patient with me, putting up with me and all my questions, and without them standing with me when everyone else left, I would still have no grasp or thought that an all-consuming love even exists.

TABLE OF CONTENTS

FOREWORD

It is interesting to write this forward, due to the fact that I have written a much more exhaustive book on this subject that has yet to be released.

This devotional came about to help people on a daily basis get established in the Biblical truths regarding the Love of God and took nearly one hundred episodes to cover on our podcast/radio show.

On a daily basis, the way we view ourselves seeks to be hi-jacked and influenced by many different voices. This makes it even more important that we hear from our Heavenly Father regarding the unconditional love He has for us and allow this love to shape every area of our lives.

The KOM family and I hope this helps you receive God's love by revelation and not just information.

We love you and believe in you.

Jesus is Risen! Victory is Assured!

Kurt Owen

BELIEVE IT, OR JUST KNOW IT?

1 John 4:16
And we have known and believed the love that God has for us. God is love, and he who abides in love abides in God, and God in him.

It is nearly impossible to go anywhere in the world and not come into contact with the simple message: "God loves you." It might be as big as a billboard or as small as a sticker on the back window of a car. It might be on a t-shirt or a TV show, but somehow you will encounter this message in almost every nation, language and people. The simple message of "God loves you" is known and seen everywhere, but rarely is it believed. Sadly, this is most often among Jesus' own people.

This is why the great Apostle John makes a distinction between knowing about the love of

God and believing that love. Especially for you personally.

The personal part is the most heartbreaking. People can be so bold and so assured of God's love for others that while witnessing to them they declare, "No matter what you have done, Jesus loves you and will receive you as His own. Your past doesn't matter. Give your life to Jesus today."

BUT, the exact same people at 2 AM when they are crying out to their Heavenly Father for help, feel the need to beg, plead and bargain with Him. This is because they don't truly believe the love God has for them.

They know about it, but they do not believe it. This problem needs to be acknowledged so that it can be attacked and corrected.

I want you to make a choice today that over the next 31 days you will begin to believe and accept God's love for you more than you ever have before. Even if you believe some of the love of God, you are going to find over these next chapters that He loves you more than you can possibly imagine. And, I trust Jesus that you will begin to believe and count on this love.

Pray this today:

Father, with all my heart, I don't want to just know about your love for me, I want to believe it with every fiber of my being. Starting today, I am asking you that as I read this devotional, you'd cause your love for me to become a heart revelation in my life personally. I know you love the world, but I NEED to know and believe that you love me. I ask you for this and choose to believe that I have received, in Jesus's name. Amen.

Now, read 1 John 4:16 several times today, and then declare boldly, "I know and believe The love Jesus has for me."

DAY 2

CAN YOU PASS THE TEST?

1 John 4:18
There is no fear in love, but perfect love casts out fear because fear involves torment. But he who fears has not been made perfect in love.

How do you know whether or not you just know about God's love, or if you know AND believe God's love for you?

Test yourself with these simple questions:

Do you constantly feel as if you must get a lot of people to pray in order to make sure you get God's help for a situation? Or, even just one person? Acting as though Jesus would not do it simply because you asked.

Have you ever tried to make a deal with God in order to secure His help? You might have said something like, "Lord, if you will do this, I will never again do (fill in the blank)," or, the reverse,

"Lord, if you will do this for me, then I will (fill in the blank)."

Have you offered glory to God in exchange for help? "Lord, if you will do this, I will glorify you to everyone." Or, similarly, "Lord, if you will do this, then people will see it and know you are truly God and glorify you."

Maybe you promised to give an offering in exchange for His help such as, "Lord, if you will do this, I will give (fill in the dollar amount) into You Kingdom."

Have you walked the floor quoting His Word to Him in an effort to convince Him of your case and need for help? Or, similarly, have you confessed His Word over and over again in order to get Him to move on your behalf?

Or, the ultimate test: Are you ever afraid of anything or anyone? You might think, "It's impossible to live free from fear!" Oh, but it is possible and believing God's love is the answer to it. 1 John 4:18 teaches His perfect love will drive out your fear.

If you have ever found yourself in one or all of these situations, you don't truly believe the love that Your Heavenly Father has for you personally.

Don't be condemned, though, we have all experienced this. We must major on knowing how much God loves us AND believing it; this is what changes our walk of faith...FOREVER.

Over these next few days together I believe that all of your fears will become less and less until they are no more. How? Because you will know intimately of Jesus' love for you, AND you will begin to trust in this perfect love. Stay with it!

Pray this today:
Father, as you know, I want to know AND believe Your love for me more than I ever have before. I believe even now that revelation of Your love for me is driving fear of any type out of me forever. I make a choice today to trust Your love for me!

FAR MORE THAN YOU THINK

Ephesians 3:19
...To know the love of Christ which passes knowledge, that you may be filled with all the fullness of God.

Most Notice here that Jesus' love for you is so extremely vast that it is beyond what your natural mind can truly grasp or understand. In other words, as you begin to see how much God loves you, you must also realize Jesus' love for you is far beyond anything you think you understand about His love.

He is so completely head over heels in love with you that He was willing to do anything to have a relationship with you and to be able to help you.

You are the apple of His eye and He has intimate knowledge of you. Everything you would ever do right, and even do wrong, He knows. Yet He has still cried out to you, "I LOVE YOU!!!"

Now, just because your natural mind in and of itself cannot fully understand His love doesn't mean you should give up on knowing it. You cannot say, "Well, if I can't know it, then what's the point; I might as well give up now if my mind cannot grasp it!" Why? Because you are not your natural mind. In truth, your mind is a part of you, but it is not the spiritual you. You are a spirit.

In your spirit, you are exactly like Jesus and able to know and believe things that might make your natural mind go tilt. You must continue to study, think about and speak out loud over and over (meditate) the scriptures that talk about your Heavenly Father's love for you.

You must also be willing to accept and continually remind yourself that no matter how much you have currently accepted Jesus' love, He loves you much, much, much, much, much, (much x ∞) more than anything you are thinking!

Speak This All Day Today:
Father, I receive and choose to believe the love you have for me. I ask you to help me to know your love for me more than I do right now. I also accept and acknowledge that right now, at this moment, you love me beyond anything I have seen or known of your love so far.

Now say this and choose to believe it! Regardless of whether or not you are having a great day or a horrible day. If you have done everything right, or if you screwed up everything, this is still true! So confess it and choose to believe it; "Father, You love ME!"

***If you have not heard our teaching on Spirit, Soul & Body, we recommend you contact us and we will help you receive a copy. This teaching is vital and will help you grow tremendously in the area of understanding the difference between your mind and your spirit.

DAY 4

WHY THIS IS IMPORTANT TO YOU

Ephesians 3:19
...To know the love of Christ which passes knowledge, that you may be filled with all the fullness of God.

Stop and think about what this verse is saying. To be filled with the fullness of God Himself does not depend on what actions you take. It simply is *knowing* and *believing* the love Jesus has for you.

Most people believe that to be filled with God you must be perfect and do everything right. However, that is not what this verse says. Rather, it shows us that in order to be filled with God you have to know and believe Jesus' love for you.

The question is: Why is your knowing and believing God's love for you the valve that determines how much you are filled with Him?

Because you will always limit what you allow God to do for you, if you don't know and believe His love for you. Now, you may be thinking, I cannot limit God... After all, He's God. Oh, but you can, and I guarantee you that to some extent, you do limit Him. Several scriptures point to this but Psalm 78:41 specifically says people can and have limited God in their lives.

Psalm 78:41
Yea, they turned back and tempted God, and limited the Holy One of Israel.

Now, why did Israel turn back? Because they did not truly understand and believe God's care and commitment to them. This led them to thinking, "Surely, God isn't this big, this good, this much in love with us!" And, what was the result? He wanted to help them more than they were willing to receive His help. God is not going to make you take Him; He loves you and will always honor your choice. If you put on the brakes, He will honor your decision.

Isn't it time we take the limits off of our Heavenly Father and allow Him to love and to fill our lives the way He has always desired?

In order to do this, you must "know the love of Christ which passes knowledge" so that you can be "filled with The Fullness of God."

Pray this today:

Father, I ask you to reveal Your love to me. Help me to know the width, the length, the depth and the height of Your love for me. I choose to believe in this love. Teach me how to quit limiting You in my life. Thank you for doing this for me, in Jesus' Name. Amen.

I strongly encourage you to revisit and complete yesterday's exercise again today.

DAY 5

DID YOU REALLY JUST TELL JESUS TO STOP?

Matthew 8:8
The Centurion answered and said, "Lord, I am not worthy that You should come under my roof. But only speak a word, and my servant will be healed."

I strongly encourage you to read Matthew 8:5-13 to understand the full context of this verse. In the meantime, I'd like to catch you up on some vital takeaways from this passage.

The Centurion asked for help. Jesus said, "I will come to your house and help." However, despite Jesus' willingness to help him, the Centurion insisted he was not worthy to have Jesus set foot under his roof.

This may seem like an oversimplification, but it is entirely accurate. Thankfully, the Centurion understood authority & had faith in Jesus' Word enough that he still received the miracle he needed.

However, the fact is, the Centurion did not allow Jesus to do what He wanted to do.

Interestingly enough, the Centurion disqualified himself from Jesus coming to his house AFTER Jesus said He would come. Jesus qualified him, but the Centurion disqualified himself. He stopped Jesus from what He wanted and was willing to do.

Who held more qualifications to judge in this scenario? Jesus or the Centurion? The obvious answer is Jesus! Yet, this man would not receive Jesus' love, care, or help.

Notice the reaction of Jesus in this situation. The Centurion thought he was unworthy and would not accept a visit, and Jesus never tried to override his thought process or will. He loved him too much to do that.

Let's make this personal and apply it to your life. Have you ever tried to disqualify yourself from a miracle after Jesus has already qualified you? Jesus himself, through His love and actions, has already qualified you. For this reason, we must know the love of Christ so that we allow ourselves to be filled with all the fullness of God.

The next time you are tempted to quote the reasons why you are unworthy, catch yourself. Don't allow unworthy feelings or apparent inadequacies to stop Jesus from doing what He wants to do. Let Him help you, exactly how He desires to help you!

Pray this today:
Father, I repent for all of the times I have focused on my apparent unworthiness after Jesus has made me worthy. I receive and accept your love for me and the price you paid to make me worthy through your death, burial, and resurrection. I receive this love. Show me where I am limiting you and help me change. In Jesus' Name, Amen.

I DIDN'T STOP HIM, I ASKED FOR HELP. WHY DIDN'T HE HELP?

Matthew 8:8
The Centurion answered and said, "Lord, I am not worthy that You should come under my roof. But only speak a word, and my servant will be healed.

I know this is the same Scripture from yesterday, and, again, I strongly encourage you to read Matthew 8:5-13 to get the context of this verse.

Many times people earnestly cry out to Jesus for help, and when help doesn't come they assume that it must not have been Jesus' will to help because He didn't come through for them.

After reading yesterday's devotional many of you may have even said, "Nope, that's not me. I have cried out, begged even, for God to help and have never limited Him."

Just because you are asking for help, (however earnest and heartfelt it may be) does not mean that on the inside you are not also disqualifying yourself from the very help for which you are asking.

Remember, in these verses the Centurion came and asked for help, too. Earnest. Heartfelt. With genuine need. The same Centurion disqualified himself from the love and help Jesus wanted and was willing to give. Just because you ask, plead, beg and have a very real need does not mean you are not also at the same time disqualifying yourself from this same help Jesus wants to give you.

Let me ask you this: Have you ever prayed and asked for something, but at the same time thought about whether you had done the 'right things' necessary to receive help from your Heavenly Father? In desperate need you may have cried out, all the while saying in your mind, "I have not read my Bible enough, confessed the Word enough, prayed enough, acted Holy enough." You were looking to see if you were qualified for His help. If you were like me, you always came up short, you began to limit what you would allow Jesus to do for you. Why? Because you did not believe that Jesus loved you more than your shortcomings.

You looked at you and not at Him. You asked for help, from someone who desperately wanted to help you, and then at the same time shut down your faith by not trusting in Jesus and His limitless love for you.

It is time to quit disqualifying yourself when your Lord's love has qualified you. It was His love for you personally that compelled Him to pay the price for your sin to remove anything that was against you. Jesus, and His love for you, is the only thing you should look at when you pray because He and His love are your only needed qualification.

Pray this today:
Father, I am sorry for any time I have tried to qualify for Your love that you have so freely poured out towards me. I make a decision today to see my trust in Jesus and what He has done for me as my only qualification for help. I will never disqualify myself again because Your help for me is not based upon my actions; it is solely based on Jesus' actions. I pray this in faith in The Name of The One who has qualified me for Your help, Jesus my Lord. Amen.

DAY 7

HAVING TROUBLE COMMITTING TO GOD'S PLANS FOR YOUR LIFE?

Mark 10:22
And he was sad at that saying, and went away grieved: for he had great possessions.

If you are having trouble totally committing to God's plan for your life, you don't truly believe The Love Jesus has for you.

I strongly encourage you to read this whole passage of scripture Mark 10:1-31 to get the complete context. Once again we have someone coming to Jesus asking for help. Help He is more than willing to give, but when He tries, the person simply will not receive it.

This man had a burning question and a sincere need. He wants eternal life. Jesus loves Him; the Scripture specifically says this. But He asks the young man to trust in Jesus' love and provision, more than the young man trusts in his own possessions and plans.

But he will not receive what The Lord is trying to do in his life. The young man thinks that he loves himself more than Jesus loves him, and that he wants better for himself than Jesus wants for him. He clearly thinks it would be better to trust himself, his care for himself and his resources rather than to trust in Jesus and His provision.

Because the young man does not believe and trust in Jesus' love for him, He counts Jesus' instructions as loss and will not commit. But Jesus was not trying to take from the young man, NO! Jesus, with His great love for the young man, wanted to fill his life.

Let's take another look at Ephesians 3:19.

Ephesians 3:19
...To know the love of Christ which passes knowledge; that you may be filled with all the fullness of God.

The young man would not allow Jesus to fill his life because He did not or would not know and believe the love Jesus had for him.

Because of His limitless love for you, anything Jesus asks you to do will bring fullness, not loss.

Make the decision to confront anything contrary to this within yourself, and choose to believe and accept His love.

Pray this today:
Heavenly Father, you want better for me than I want for myself. Show me by your Spirit when I am going against your plan for my life, and I will make a change. I choose to trust Your love for me! You are for me and not against me. Your desire is to give me a rich, full life. Thank you for revealing Your love for me more and more each day. In Jesus' Name, Amen.

YOU SHOULD DOUBT YOUR LOVE FOR GOD

1 John 4:19
We love Him because He first loved us.

Most people exist in a strange reverse when it comes to The Love of God. They are completely convinced of their love for God. I have even had people living in absolute unrepentant sin tell me, "I love God."

If I were to question their love for Jesus, they would immediately attack: "Who do you think you are to question my love for God? How dare you!!! I certainly do love God, and it is horrible that you would imply anything different."

Yet, for most of these same people, if I said, "God doesn't love you!," the response might be "I know it. How could He? After everything that I have done."

They are totally convinced of their love for Jesus, but so very shaky and uncertain about His love for them. This is the exact reverse of reality. If you doubt anything, it should be your love for Him; NEVER EVER should you doubt His Love for you.

Why? Because any love you have for Him is only possible because He loved you first. Your love testifies and is proof He loves you.

No matter how much you think you love Him, Jesus loved you first and more! More than you could possibly know.

No matter how convinced you are of your love for Him, you must be more convinced of His love for you. Your love is only made possible by His love for you.

He is in love with you!

Today, say this to yourself over and over:
I love Jesus, and I am only able to love Him because He first loved me. I receive my Heavenly Father's love for me because I love Him and His love made my love possible. I love Jesus, and Jesus is head over heels in love with me! I refuse to doubt Jesus' love for me.

HE LOVED YOU BEFORE YOU EVER THOUGHT ABOUT HIM

1 John 4:19
We love Him because He first loved us.

Jesus loved you from the very beginning. He knew everything you would ever do, even the vilest of actions that you have taken or will take, and He loved you anyway.

As we saw yesterday, Jesus did not love you because you first loved Him; the reverse is actually true. You love Him because He loved you first.

Think about it! Jesus' love for you was not in response to you loving Him, nor was Jesus' love for you in response to any action you took. No, Jesus' love for you was not the response to anything you did or did not do. And it still isn't!

If you blew it yesterday, Jesus' love for you did not change. Why? Because Jesus was not responding to you when He chose to love you.

Jesus loves you for who you are, not what you do. You cannot do anything to get Jesus to love you more, and you can't do anything to get Jesus to love you less. His love for you is not based on your doing, it is based on His choosing, and He chose you. Why? Because He loves you.

Does this mean you should go ahead and sin because Jesus is still going to love you regardless? No, because then you would be exploiting His love and using His Love against Him. Sin is the action of someone moving away from Jesus, not moving towards Him. It is also the action of a person who wants sin more than they want Him, and love themselves more than they love Him.

I don't believe this is you, nor do I believe you want this to be you. If that were the case, you wouldn't be taking the time to read this. However, you will make some mistakes along the way, because we all do! And when you sin, run to Jesus, not from Him. Why? Because He is hopelessly in love with you and wants to help you be free from sin.

How can you be sure of this? Because His love was not a response to any action you took. He did not choose to love you because you got it right, so His love doesn't stop when you get it wrong. He loved you first because He wanted to and that has not changed.

Say this over and over today:
Jesus, I love you and want to love you more. No matter how many mistakes I make or sins I commit, I will not run from you. I will run to You and receive your help to change. I refuse condemnation in all forms because you love me. I will rest in that love today.

THE JUDGMENT OF GOD. GOOD OR BAD?

1 John 4:17
Love has been perfected among us in this: that we may have boldness in the day of judgment; because as He is, so are we in this world.

Most people are terrified of God's judgment. In fact, many have been threatened by others with the judgment of God. People say things like, "God is going to judge you for that." To top it off, we often face fear in our own heads, thinking we cannot run to Jesus when we sin, in fear of His reaction to our choice.

This thinking and theology is the exact opposite of the way it should be.

We should not fear Jesus and His judgment by running away from it, but rather embrace it with boldness.

Does this mean that because Jesus, the Judge of All Creation, is for us we simply get a pass? No, not at all. Jesus is The Righteous, Just Judge.

However, all of His judgments are for our good. He is not against us! His judgment is meant to show us the most fulfilling, highest ways of just living, so we can receive all that He has for us.

When you sin and make a mistake, don't run from Jesus. Run to Jesus! Run to Him because even His judgment for you is good. He loves you so much that His judgments are tempered with His Love and Mercy.

In The Old Testament, The Ark of The Covenant contained the Ten Commandments inside. These tablets gave rules by which God would judge humanity. Even then, in an age where the law ruled, above the tablets rested the mercy seat. God looked down at the commandments, and He saw them through mercy.

If you have made mistakes and messed up terribly, or even just a little, don't fear and run from the judgment of God. Instead, choose to embrace the fact that the judgment of God is meant to give you the very best life possible. Run into the open arms of a God that loves you more than He hates your sin.

Pray this today:
Father, without fear I come before you and ask you to judge me. I know you love me, and your judgment is only for my good. I refuse to fear you, a God that loves me so much. Please show me where I may have missed your best plan for my life through wrong actions, words, or thoughts that are holding me back. I choose to trust you. Thank you for helping me change. In Jesus' Name! Amen!

I REFUSE TO FEAR GOD!

1 John 4:18
There is no fear in love, but perfect love casts out fear because fear involves torment. But he who fears has not been made perfect in love.

I refuse to fear God!

Is this a radical statement to you?

Are you willing to say it for yourself?

The only way you can truly make this statement is if you are absolutely convinced of God's love for you. Knowing, believing, and accepting His love for you should drive all fear out of your life. Especially any wrong fear of Him!

Why should you have a negative fear of someone who is completely in love with you? Someone who only wants your good, you blessed, and your satisfaction in life.

The unconditional love of God should free you from all fear. Considering that the God of the

Universe loves you more than everyone else on the face of this earth, He should be the last person you are afraid of encountering.

In yesterday's devotional, we talked about the verse right before this one, concerning God's judgment. Notice the progression of these verses; you should be bold before God and His judgment without fear, knowing the One judging you is also the One who loves you. This knowledge of love should drive out all fear of judgment.

Also, take notice of WHY Jesus doesn't want you to be afraid. Because fear will cause you to be tormented and Jesus doesn't want that for you, His child. If you fear God, it is because you do not honestly believe He loves you. Choose to believe and accept His love for you today!

Some may mistakenly think that I don't believe in "the fear of the Lord" as mentioned in several places in The New Testament. This is absolutely NOT true. In fact, I am believing in a revival of the fear of The Lord across the globe. The difference lies in the definition of terms.

I believe that every believer should live in a fear of The Lord, defined as an ever-increasing awestruck wonder and abiding overwhelming reverence for

God our Father, and Jesus Christ our Lord. I DO NOT believe that we should be afraid of them. It would be extremely difficult to, "Come boldly to the throne of grace, that we may obtain mercy and find grace to help in time of need" (Hebrews 4:16) if you are terrified of them.

This chapter, taken in the context of the entire book, should make this position clear. But in the event, this shocking title leads you to believe that I don't believe in the reverential fear of the Lord, you are mistaken. This chapter is designed to get people to run to Jesus and not from Him. In fact, it is my heartfelt belief, and my experience that the more you understand what Jesus has done for you and how much He loves you, the more your reverence for Him should increase.

Further, let me say to those who consider themselves spiritual but do not have Jesus as their Lord, you should be terrified of facing God. Because apart from Jesus, you have no hope in the day of judgment. And that... should be terrifying to you. You need Jesus!

Pray this today:

Father God, I refuse to be afraid of you! I have no reason to be afraid of you because you love me completely. Of all the things in life, being afraid of you is the last thing I should do, and I refuse to do it! You love me, and I have no reason to be afraid of you, for you only desire good for me. I ask You to reveal your love for me in a greater measure. I love you, honor you, and revere you, but I refuse to be afraid of you. Instead, I will believe and trust in Your love each and every day. In Jesus Name! Amen.

Day 12

I REFUSE TO FEAR...
ANYTHING!!

1 John 4:18-19
There is no fear in love, but perfect love casts out fear because fear involves torment. But he who fears has not been made perfect in love. We love Him because He first loved us.

In the last two days, we have uncovered the following:

- We should not fear the judgment of God.
  AND
- We should not fear God Himself.

Why? Because God loves us perfectly and completely.

The question then becomes: If God loves us, is there anything to fear?

Well, let's first establish who is this God that loves us so completely? He is not just God; He is ALMIGHTY God. He has all power, all knowledge and is all present. He has all of these attributes and yet loves you perfectly. He has unlimited love for you and is willing to use all of His power and knowledge on your behalf.

If you have access to all of God's power, knowledge, and resources, is there anything worthy of fear?

People? Nope. There is no one bigger, stronger, or more powerful than Jesus.

Debt? Nope. The riches of Heaven belong to you.

Sickness? Nope. Jesus, our Divine Healer, bore our sickness and carried our diseases.

Accidents? Nope. His perfect love will warn you. Just stay sensitive to His leading, then listen and follow His instruction.

Fear is just an indicator that you have not yet believed the love God has for you. Regardless of the problem, nothing is bigger than Jesus and His love for you.

Meditate on His love.
Believe it.
Accept it.

Allow it to permeate the very core of your being.

Then you will have the confidence to declare, "I will not fear, because I HAVE been made perfect in love."

Confess this today:
Fear, in The Name of Jesus, I command you to go! Leave me now! From this moment forward, I refuse to fear. I have no reason to fear! Almighty God is in love with me and wants to help me in every area of my life. I trust in God's love for me TODAY!

DAY 13

WHOSE SIDE ARE YOU ON ANYWAY?

Psalm 118:6
The Lord is on my side; I will not fear: what can man do unto me?

It's pretty straightforward, isn't it? If Almighty God is on your side, there is nothing to fear. What can man, life, even the devil himself, seek to do to you that is bigger than Jesus? Nothing!

Notice here the Psalmist is making a choice of His will when he declares, "I WILL not fear." He looked at everything and everyone that was against him and still chose not to fear.

This was not an attempt to be brave or to gut it out. No! He was looking at Almighty God, and this caused him to be empowered to live a fear-free life. By concentrating, meditating and considering The Lord, he chose the freedom of love and refused the temptation to fear.

We now know that the Psalmist chose not to fear, but did you also catch the "why" behind his choice? Because The Lord of Glory & Might was on his side!

The Lord's love for you is deeply intimate, personal, and has nothing to do with your own merit.

The man who wrote this Psalm wasn't perfect. He was a man. An unborn-again man at that. (No one could be born again until after Jesus was raised from the dead). He was not even God's child like you are. No, he was an imperfect man who likely made many mistakes. But he was still able to refuse fear because he knew The One on his side was greater than any of his mistakes. All his fears evaporated in the presence and knowledge of the God who loved him.

God is not just out wandering around the universe; nor is He sitting staring at you struggling in your problems as though you are His science experiment. Above all, you must settle in your heart that He loves you and is on your side.

Your heart will become established and settled when you intentionally set your focus and meditate on the Love of God. Take the time needed to renew your mind to His love for you. Confess it out loud and roll it over and over in your mind.

Jesus is on your side; therefore, you have no reason to fear!

Pray this today:
Lord, Your Word says that you are on my side. You are not against me; you are for me. You've done everything needed for me to be victorious, and you have withheld nothing. Because you are on my side, I refuse to fear! Fear, GO! The resources of Almighty God are mine, and there is no problem bigger than my God. Jesus is on my side; therefore, I refuse to fear!

DAY 14

THIS? AGAIN?!

Romans 8:31
What then shall we say to these things? If God is for us, who can be against us?

Are you noticing a theme over the last couple of days? God is for you!

If He is for you, then who can be against you? Another translation says it this way: "If God is for you, who can successfully be against you?"

Attacks will come, but if you trust the One who loves you and cooperate with Him, no attack can succeed. Or to paraphrase Isaiah, the weapon may be formed, but it will not prosper against you.

Paul believes God is for him. In fact, Paul is counting on the fact that God is for him. He has faith in God's love and commitment to him. Paul sees his life's challenges through the filter of God being for him. And you know what? The problems are found wanting. They simply aren't bigger than Jesus.

Why does this matter? Because these problems you face are not only against you, they are against Jesus as well. Jesus is for you and is on your side!

Think about it! Of all the problems you face, if Jesus was facing them, would they be an issue for Him? No, they would not. Therefore, since Jesus is on your side and for you, they are no problem for you either because you and Jesus are against them together.

Don't run from your problems today or stick your head in the sand. Look at them square in the face! Get a good look. Which of them is bigger than Jesus? If the answer is none (and it should be!), then you should have confidence and boldness knowing the victory belongs to you. Why? Because Jesus is for you!

Also, think about this; because God is for you His plan for you is only good. Why run or be hesitant about committing to Jesus' plan for your life, when He is committed to your good in all things?

God is not against you and has never been. God is for you and wants to help give you a better life.

Why? Because He is in love with you and that's what people who are in love do.

Say this today:
Problems, debts, sickness, future (name anything that is weighing on you or that you face) you no longer rule over me. I no longer fear you. Jesus is for me, and you cannot successfully be against me. I break your power over me in Jesus' name.

Jesus, I commit to your plan for my life. You are for me; therefore, I no longer fear what you may ask me to do. Make clear to me your will, and I will do it. I will follow you because you are for me.

DAY 15

GOD: PROBLEM MAKER OR PROBLEM SOLVER?

Isaiah 54:15
Indeed, they shall surely assemble, but not because of Me.
Whoever assembles against you shall fall for your sake.

We all have problems. We all have attacks on our lives. No matter how blessed you are, no matter how closely you follow Jesus, you will have problems. However, problems are not the issue.

The issue is the shocking amount of time God is blamed for the bad things happening. Common statements you hear concerning this are:

"Why did God do this?"
"What is God trying to teach me?"
"Why is God allowing this to happen?"
"Why isn't God doing something?"

Yet, those same people never look at themselves, their choices, the devil, or the fact that there is a curse operating in the earth.

Marcus, who is like a son to me, said to me once, "Why is it when problems come, people blame the only One who is perfect in the situation?"

God is explicitly telling us in this verse, "There will be attacks, but not because of Me." He goes on to assure us that He will cause our problems to fall before us. God is not the problem; He is the author of the solution to the problem.

And why will your problems fall before you? Because of some grand design? No, for a very personal reason. For your sake. He will do it for you because He is in love with you.

Thinking God is somehow responsible for your problem is not only wrong, but it is also a sign you either don't know or believe how much He loves you.

What is Jesus trying to help you see in this verse? You will have problems, yes. But He is not the cause of your problems. Not only that but, if you look to Him and trust in His unfailing love for you, these problems, no matter how great, will fall before you.

Refuse to believe the lie that God is your problem. It will hinder you in every way and corrupt your faith. We will dive into this deeper in tomorrow's devotional.

Pray this today:
Father, I repent to you for even considering that you were at fault. I repent for even thinking that somehow, someway, you were to blame for my problems. I know that you love me, and are not the source of my problems. Your desire is only for my good and to help me. Teach me how to walk in my authority and possess all that you have freely done for me.

Confess this today:
Problems, you listen to me, in The Name of Jesus, you fall before me now! It is the will of my Father God. Amen!!

DAY 16

WOULD YOU ASK FOR HELP FROM THE ONE CHOKING YOU?

Isaiah 54:15
Indeed, they shall surely assemble, but not because of Me.
Whoever assembles against you shall fall for your sake.

Faith will always be difficult if you think God is the cause of your problem. You may want to argue that fact, but let me ask you a question.

If I grab you by the throat and begin to choke the life out of you, would you ask me (the one choking you!) for help? Or better yet, could you have confidence or any real trust that if I am the one hurting you that I would also be the one to help you? Of course not! You'd conclude really quick that if I wanted to help you, I wouldn't be choking you in the first place.

In that same way, if you think God is causing your life's challenges, you cannot truly, deep down trust Him to help you.

God is making it clear in this verse; I am not the problem creator; I am the problem solver. It is pointless to ask, "God, why did you..." because He didn't. He is trying to express how much He loves you and wants to help, not to harm.

If you can relate to blaming God for your problem, whether in your mind or out loud, that is an indicator of why you are having difficulty trusting & believing. Ultimately, it is an indicator of a lack of belief in Jesus' love for you.

Begin to meditate on the fact that Jesus is your Helper, not your abuser. He is The One who loves you and is seeking out ways to bless you.

Problems will come, but not from Jesus. He will cause your problems to fall before you because He loves you.

Do you find this message I am saying repetitive? Well, it is. And it needs to be. The reality is that blaming God for problems is something I am continually hearing people say. It is continuously being spoken because it is continually being thought.

Determine today (and every day!) that any thoughts of God being your problem will be countered with this confession:

"Jesus is helping me right now. He has nothing to do with the cause of my challenges. Problems will come, but not because of Him. I worship and thank you, Lord, that right now You are causing my problems to fall before me. You are my source of deliverance. Thank you for delivering me, honoring me, and showing me your salvation."

In fact, don't wait for a thought to come; confess it out loud right now!

DAY 17

GOD IS NOT IN CONTROL

...

OR IS HE?

Genesis 1:26
Then God said, "Let Us make man in Our image,
according to Our likeness; let them have dominion over the
fish of the sea, over the birds of the air, and over the cattle,
over all the earth and over every creeping thing that creeps
on the earth."

It is a common misconception that God is in control of everything that happens in the earth; that nothing occurs unless God causes it or, at the very least, allows it.

If this were true, then there is a very logical question that needs to follow: If God is a good God who loves us so much, then why is this world so evil? Children are starving, children are born with horrible birth defects, and the atrocities that happen daily in the world are beyond imagination.

If God is in control, and God is so loving, why do these things happen?

The answer is simply this: God is NOT in control. At least, not the way most people imagine.

In Genesis 1:26, at the very beginning of creation, God gives his man, Adam, dominion (control) over this planet.

From that moment on, it is man who is responsible for everything that happens. It is not that God was not willing to help Adam, but Adam had a right to choose whether or not he would obey God.

There is much more I could say about this, but this is still true today. Prove it out in your own life. Has God ever told you, "Don't say that," and you said it anyway? How did that turn out for you? (I imagine rather badly.) Or, has He ever told you to do something and you chose not to listen and then afterward said to yourself, "Ohhh, that's why He wanted me to do that!"

If you have walked with Jesus for any length of time, then you likely answered, "Yes" to both of those scenarios. What does this prove? It proves that God is not even in control of you! If He were, you would have made a different decision than you did. But, because you had dominion, you had the choice to say, "No."

God is not in control of you unless you yield to Him. And Adam did not yield to God. The devil, sin, and death have run loose in the earth since that day. All because the one who had dominion and control yielded to sin rather than The Author of every good and perfect gift. (James 1:17)

Who will you choose to yield to today?

Pray this today:
Father, I repent for ever blaming you for any evil in the world and in particular in my life. You are the Author of every good and perfect gift, not evil and death. I choose to yield to you today. Your only desire is for my good and to be good to me. I acknowledge and yield to your counsel and plan for my life. Once I know it is you, I will respond positively without hesitation. Help me to keep this commitment, in Jesus' name!

Your answers are there, on the inside of you. Jesus wants you to have them, but you will need to give it some time.

DAY 18

HOW CAN GOD BE LOVE AND CAUSE THIS PAIN?

Genesis 2:15-17
The Lord God took the man and put him in the garden of
Eden to tend and keep it. And the Lord God commanded
the man, saying, "Of every tree of the garden you may
freely eat; but of the tree of the knowledge of good and evil
you shall not eat, for in the day that you eat of it you shall
surely die."

What we are about to discuss is crucial for your faith. A lack of understanding in this topic has caused many people to go from faith in Jesus to questioning God's existence. You need to settle with finality this question in yourself and be able to answer it for others. If not, you will be vulnerable to the deception of the devil.

For example; there is nothing quite as heartbreaking as witnessing the suffering of a child. And there is a tendency to say or think, "If God is real and He is so good, why doesn't He stop this? Why does

He allow this? Every decent moral person would stop this if they could, so why does God allow/cause birth defects, sickness…(fill in the blank)?"

God did not cause birth defects, sickness and all of the other horrible things we see; we did.

Our great, great, great, great (times a bunch!) grandfather was given dominion and given a choice. He was told there was a tree that contained the knowledge of evil. Now you might say, "Actually Kurt, it was the tree of the knowledge of good and evil." But Adam already had the knowledge of good. EVERYTHING they could see, feel, and touch was good. So all they gained by eating was the knowledge of evil. Naturally, this caused death.

God never wanted man to have any knowledge or experience with evil or death. He warned Adam how they could avoid both. If man were ever going to experience death and destruction, it would be his choice, not God's.

BUT Granddaddy chose to ignore a Loving God who had freely given him everything good and instead chose to embrace evil, hurt, death and every variation of it; including birth defects. It was never God's intention for those things to exist.

Granddaddy brought birth defects and every other evil thing that exists!

Today, tune your ear to a God and Father who is completely in love with you. A God who never desires for you to experience hurt or destruction, and whose only intention is for your good.

Will you take His counsel and choose His way?

Say this today!
"I choose to follow Jesus! Jesus is in love with me and only desires my good! His every instruction is for my benefit! He guides me away from all evil, hurt, and destruction. I choose to follow you, Jesus, and experience a better life than I have ever dreamed possible. You have blessed me, and I am blessed.

DAY 19

IF GOD IS LOVE, WHY DO PEOPLE STARVE?

Genesis 1:26
Then God said, "Let Us make man in Our image, according to Our likeness; let them have dominion over the fish of the sea, over the birds of the air, and over the cattle, over all the earth and over every creeping thing that creeps on the earth."

Years ago, I was traveling and preaching throughout the midwest United States.

In one particular city I visited, I saw stacks upon stacks of grain rotting in the fields. I asked a local resident why such a viable food source was voluntarily being wasted.

This local man then went on to explain that the United States Government paid the farmers not to sell their grain at the market. Why? Because an abundance of grain sold would drive the price down both within the United States and around the world. Since that time, I have heard similar stories about other food sources. This is true in similar fashion all around the world, not just by governments but by businesses as well.

God, (who is love) is not the one causing people to starve, WE ARE! He would never do such a thing! If you go back to the very beginning in Genesis, you will see that in his love, he freely provided an abundance. Even before we were ever created, Jesus provided everything man would ever need. So what happened?

After the creation of man, he was given two vital things to succeed: Dominion and seed. Adam then became the one in charge of everything that happened on the earth. And what did he decide? Adam decided he wanted sin, death, and satan more than he wanted righteousness, life, and God. Following Adam, man began to decide money was more important than people. Further still, others decided that walking in dominion and planting seeds was too much work. Therefore, people began to starve.

Starving people are not God's doing; it is a result of man's choices. Since we have dominion over the earth, God honors our choice; even though it is against His heart.

Your Heavenly Father loves you and is for you. Before you were ever born, His Grace and Love provided everything you would ever need for life and godliness. When we begin to trust in His love and walk by faith, everything His grace provided begins to show up. When it does, we are taken care of and then have an abundance left over to share with others.

Pray this today!
Father, I see now the lack & suffering in this world is not caused by you. From the very beginning, your plan was complete abundance. Lord, I thank you that you love me and have already provided everything that pertains to life and godliness. Teach me how to walk in it! I thank you that the overflowing abundance you've given me provides more than enough for me to be generous, feed others, and fund your kingdom. In Jesus' Name, I am blessed, and I am a blessing!

DAY 20

GRANDDADDY BROUGHT
THE PAIN!

Genesis 2:15-17
"Then the Lord God took the man and put him in the garden of Eden to tend and keep it. And the Lord God commanded the man, saying, "Of every tree of the garden you may freely eat; but of the tree of the knowledge of good and evil you shall not eat, for in the day that you eat of it you shall surely die."

Up until this point, we have discussed the symptoms of this, but let's face the main question head-on:

If God is 100% Good and 100% Love, why is there evil in the world?

In the beginning, before man ever breathed his first breath, the scripture is clear that everything (EVERYTHING!) was good. It was only after man took dominion that he experienced anything other than good.

This means when God was in charge and had dominion over the earth, everything was good. Why is that? Obviously, it was only good because good was all that God ever intended for man.

Then God gave the good and perfect gift of the earth and fullness to man. In His love, God even warned man how to avoid evil, death, and hurt. His intention was for man never to experience hardship. But man took his dominion and trusted a serpent more than He trusted God.

Man's trust in the serpent came from him believing the lie that God was somehow holding out on him. Adam's ability to fall for the deceit of the serpent was due to him not understanding or trusting God's love for him. Since God freely gave everything to man, walking and talking with him daily, it appears that Adam did not believe God's love for him. Therefore, because Granddaddy Adam did not believe and trust in God's love, he made a choice that caused 100% of the evil in the world today.

Evil on the earth was Adam's choice, not God's choice.

God is 100% Good and 100% Love.

Pray this today:

Father, in The Name of Jesus, I see that you never wanted me to know evil or suffering. From the very beginning, you only wanted good for me. My Granddaddy Adam is to blame for all of the evil in the world, not you. You are Love, and your will from the beginning was only good for me. I choose to believe and trust your love for me. You would never withhold anything good from me. I choose to listen and obey because you only want good for me. Today will be a good day because you love me!

DAY 21

YOU CAN WHIP ANYTHING BECAUSE HE LOVES YOU

Romans 8:37
"Yet in all these things, we are more than conquerors through Him who loved us."

It can be a challenging concept to grasp that Jesus truly wants us to succeed and is 100% for our good. But it is true! As followers of Christ, we are called not only to conquer life's challenges but to be MORE than a conqueror. This is not only about surviving life's problems, but being able to stand completely victorious on the other side of them. Problems tend to come one of two ways; hard and fast, or so slow you feel like they are camped out permanently and will never end.

When this happens, it is very tempting to go into survival mode, adopting an attitude of "I just hope I survive!" That is not Jesus' best for you!

God is not the God of just enough to survive! He is the God of MORE than enough! And He is completely in love with you.

Just look throughout the Bible, and you will see what I am saying! When one angel, (who has been known to lay waste to tens of thousands) would be sufficient to handle a problem, does God send just one? No way! He sends an army!

Please understand, when you look at your life and see nothing but problems, God will empower you to thrive in them! He will even set a table for you in the middle of your enemies. Why? Because He is in love with you!

If you love someone, don't you want them to succeed? Of course, you do! Because you love them and that's what love does.

Notice in our key scripture that Paul brings a relationship between our winning and His loving. You can plainly see here, in His love, God has made a way for you to win! God will help you because He is in love with you! The resources of heaven are yours; therefore, you can be more than a conqueror.

If you desire to be victorious, choose to trust Jesus' love for you and every promise His love has made.

Say this today!

"I choose to trust Jesus' love for me. I am more than a conqueror through Jesus, who is completely in love with me! Problems, I will not just survive you; I will more than conquer you through Jesus Who loves me completely! Not only that, on my way to victory, I will thrive because my Lord, who loves me, is setting a table before me in the presence of my problems and enemies. The Lord is taking excellent care of me, even in the midst of my problems. Thank you, Father, for loving me! Your love promises are causing me to win over every problem because Jesus lives in me!"

GOD LOVES YOU, EVEN AT YOUR WORST

John 3:16
"For God so loved the world that He gave His only begotten Son, that whoever believes in Him should not perish but have everlasting life."

Most people who have had even the most minimal exposure to Christianity and Jesus know John 3:16. People have signs at sporting events, players write it on their faces, billboards display it; you name it, someone has probably written John 3:16 on it.

What is interesting is how many people don't truly and genuinely believe it. The general mentality among most people is that God will help you when you do good, but you are on your own when you behave poorly. Some even go as far as to say that God will not help you until you get sin out of your life. Or even worse, that God doesn't love you when you are in sin.

The funny thing is they will still put John 3:16 on anything and everything they can find! And that verse is proof that what they're saying is completely wrong.

John 3:16 is about God sending us help when we were at our worst! We were sinners, serving our flesh and carnal nature. We were not His children, and we were not looking for Him.

When our very nature was sin, and our lifestyle was yielded entirely to sin, God loved us so intensely that He sent help beyond what we could ask or think. He helped us so perfectly, and it was beyond anything we would ever need again. The most significant release of help and power the world has ever known was given to you when you were the enemy of God and lost in sin. God so loved you and this sin-ridden world that when you were at your worst, He gave you His best — asking nothing in return, except your belief in Jesus, who is Love.

Simply by believing in Jesus, sin lost control over you, and you became recreated in Him. And He did all of this when you were in sin! You weren't even His child when you were in this sin ridden state. In fact, you were His enemy, yet Jesus died for you.

So let me ask you...

What makes you think He won't help you now?

Now you are His child! You are His family!

God is in love with you and will help you right now, no matter where you are, no matter what mistakes you may have made! Newsflash, you will never be able to come out of sin and walk free from it without His help. Whatever mistakes you have made or will make, allow Jesus to help you.

Pray this today:
"Father, I see that Your love for me never changes. Even when I am at my worst, nothing can separate me from your love. Even when I sin, you never give up on me, and you will help as I continue to grow and change. Lord, I will no longer permit my mistakes to separate me from you. And since you love me this much, I don't want to sin anymore. I want to love and live like Jesus. Teach me how to do this, Father. No matter what mistakes I have made, I know you will help me today because you love me. I also commit to never take your love for granted and use your love against you by choosing a lifestyle of sin. My faith is in you, Jesus. Amen."

GOD DOES NOT WANT TO CONDEMN US

John 3:17
"For God did not send His Son into the world to condemn the world, but that the world through Him might be saved."

This verse is a favorite to my wife, Terry, as it shows God's heart of mercy towards us. However, most times, you will find God's people preaching against the very message this verse is trying to get across. We have all seen the people who think it's their mission in life to preach the condemnation of God. Whether on the TV, radio, on the streets, or even at funerals, they will blast about God's condemnation concerning them, their lifestyle and their choices.

And yet we see here that Jesus did not come into the world to condemn the world, but to save it. Have you noticed that Jesus was never a big condemner? He didn't spend a lot of time trying to make people feel like dirt for what they had done wrong.

First, we need to quit condemning God's people.

Secondly, we need to eliminate condemnation from our lives and refuse to allow it to continue stealing our faith.

There are far too many of God's children who have long since repented and yet still remain condemned. This steals their confidence towards Jesus and contaminates their faith.

The sad truth is that even though they have repented, they continue to beat themselves up over something Jesus himself doesn't remember.

Hear me! Jesus didn't come into the world to condemn you; He came to save you! It's time to start allowing Him to do what He came to do.

No, I am not just talking to those who have not accepted Jesus. I am speaking to my Christian brothers and sisters who need to go on in life.

Who need help with life's problems.

Who need their faith at full-functioning capability, yet they can't get over the past.

Jesus wants to save you; He has no interest in condemning you. He loves you and wants to help!

Pray this today:

"Lord Jesus, reveal to me by Your Spirit where I have allowed condemnation to come in. Show me these areas and help me address them. You came to save me not condemn me, and if it is not of you, I will not have it in my life anymore! I command condemnation to go now! I refuse you condemnation! My Lord loves me so much He came to save me, not condemn me. I receive the fullness of His salvation for me right here and right now! In Jesus' Name, Amen!"

GOD DID NOT SAVE YOU BECAUSE OF MERCY

Ephesians 2:4
"But God, who is rich in mercy, because of His great love with which He loved us..."

I hear people say quite frequently, "God in His infinite mercy saved us." And though I believe that mercy was involved, is His mercy what motivated Him to save us?

Have you ever thought about the fact that mercy can be extremely impersonal? Some people are merciful to others simply because they are mercy minded or merciful by nature.

Have you ever shown mercy to someone in traffic? You let them in when you didn't have to, and they certainly didn't deserve it? Did you care about them at all? Did you let them in because of who they were to you or simply because that is the type of person you are? Unless you knew them, it was because of the person you are.

Mercy can be very impersonal. But your Heavenly Father did not save you because of mercy; He saved you because He is in love with you.

And His love for you is extremely personal!

He wanted you.
He came looking for you.
He gave His very best for you.

Is God merciful to you? Absolutely! It is part of who He is. He is rich in mercy. BUT His Mercy toward you is a manifestation of His overwhelmingly personal love for you, not some impersonal characteristic of His.

God knows every hair on your head; He knows every tear, every thought... Why? Because you are extremely important to Him. Jesus is in love with you!

God saved you because He loved and wanted you; not just because He is merciful by nature.

Say this today!
"Father, I am very grateful for your Mercy. I am thankful for your mercy towards me, which is new every day! I see now, though, that your love towards me is the motivation of your mercy towards me.

Your love for me is not a concept or religious idea; no, it is a personal thing with you. You love me, personally. You care about me individually. Thank you, Lord. I love you, too! Help me today not to love you by concept or religious idea but in an intimate, personal way, as you love me. That's what I want, Father, so please help me. In Jesus' Name, Amen."

IN TIMES OF FAILURE, YOU STILL HAVE ACCESS TO GOD'S BEST

Luke 15:22
"But the father said to his servants, 'Bring forth the best robe, and put it on him; and put a ring on his hand, and shoes on his feet.'"

If you are anything like me, you end up needing God's help the most on days when you have been a real meathead. On those less than stellar days, I realized I needed to repent, and I suspect you felt the same way. While kicking yourself in condemnation and wondering how you could be so stupid, you cry out to God for help.

It's tempting to have the thought of, "How long will I have to be good before God will help me?" Fortunately, He answered that question for you in Luke 15:11-31.

Let me give you a brief idea of what this story in Luke is all about. Refusing to listen to his father, the younger son completely blew his entire inheritance on reckless living. The son is now broke, starving, and has decided to head home in the hope that his father will make him like one of his hired servants so he can at least have a meal.

What does the father do? Seeing him afar off, he runs to him. He doesn't wait for the son to tell him how sorry he is or to listen to his son's sad speech about how he is willing to be a servant. No, he immediately embraces him, puts a robe around his body and the family ring on his finger. The father gives the son the very best that he has. The Bible even specifies that the father gave him the BEST robe. I encourage you to read the whole passage several times to let it sink deep into your heart.

What is Jesus trying to say through all of this?

God has no interest in hearing what a worm you are or how terrible your behavior has been. You turning around and coming home is evidence enough of your change of heart. He is not waiting to help you. NO! He is giving you His very best, right away!

Why would He act like this? Because He loves you that much!! He is not withholding from you even when you screw up. If you are willing to turn around, His best is available to you right now.

He loves you more than He hates your sin.

Pray this today:
Lord, I am so grateful no matter the mistakes I make, you will never turn me away when I want to come home. You are not impressed with my groveling; you just want me home, and it is enough when I turn around and come to you. Your very best is available to me, RIGHT NOW! You want to help me; you are not willing to cast me aside. You want me, and I want You. I love You, and I will never use Your love against You with a lifestyle of sin. I do not desire to hurt you after all of the love that you have shown me. All I desire is to fully love you back & act in a way that is pleasing to you. You are not a withholder; you are a generous giver. Jesus, you are my Lord, and I am yours. Thank you for blessing me and helping me today.

DAY 26

RUN TO JESUS, NOT FROM HIM

John 8:10
"When Jesus had raised Himself up and saw no one but the woman, He said to her, 'Woman, where are those accusers of yours? Has no one condemned you?'"

If you read through this entire passage in John 8:1-12, you will notice how Jesus treats you when you sin.

Here is a woman who was caught in adultery, and it states, "In the very act." That implies they brought her directly from the bed to the church!

This woman wasn't at church to get her life right. She didn't even choose to come to church by an act of her will. She was brought, dragged from the bed of sin to the church.

These religious men did not care about this woman. She was simply a means to an end. She wasn't a person to them; she was a "such." She was used as a weapon against Jesus in front of the entire crowd at church that day. Her religious accusers didn't care about sin, because if they had, they would have brought the man committing adultery with her. After all, they dragged her from "the very act," so the man would have been available to pull as well.

The woman is brought alone, with likely just the sheet from the bed with which she came. But notice Jesus' response. While the religious accusers were conscious of the crowd, Jesus rises and sees no one but her.

He doesn't care what the crowd thinks. He sees only this hurting woman, in sin and abused by religion. Does He condemn her and try to make her feel like dirt for what she JUST did? No! He gives her 100% of His focus, letting her know, "Hey, I am not your accuser. I am your Savior."

As you read on, you will notice that He does not excuse her behavior either. He states it for what it is; sin. But her sin does not keep Him from loving her and desiring to help.

He does, however, warn her that if she keeps this sin in her life, it will destroy her. He doesn't accuse or condemn, but simply reminds her of the fact that choosing this life of sin will destroy you.

Remember, sin will destroy you, even if you have met Jesus.

Notice also that the woman doesn't run off at her first chance. This love from Jesus has gotten her attention. She calls Him "Lord" and stays with Him. Love will cause that reaction.

When you make a mistake, don't run from Jesus, run to Him. He doesn't want to beat you and make you feel like trash. He wants to save you, even if you have caused the problems you are facing. He will give you his attention and show you a path to walk free.

Pray this today:
"Jesus, thank you for loving me. I commit today to never run from you when I sin, but rather to you. You don't want to condemn me; you want to save me, even from the problems I have created. I choose you and your ways over the devil and his ways. When I make a mistake, I will run to you quickly and not wait for destruction to show up. I don't want sin; I want you!"

And if you have sin in your life right now, why wait? Run to Jesus right now!

DON'T FEEL BAD, JUST CHANGE

John 8:11
"And Jesus said to her, 'Neither do I condemn you; go and sin no more.'"

Even when you've repented, some people act like it is their God-given mission to guilt you for your mistakes, especially if you've wronged them.

Don't misunderstand what I am saying; if you are a child of God and you've sinned, you should feel remorseful. Godly sorrow works repentance. (2 Corinthians 7:10) Acting in sin is in direct conflict with your identity in Christ. Remember, you are the very righteousness of God in Christ Jesus. The nature of God is who you are.

While Godly sorrow works repentance, worldly sorrow seeks to condemn you and make you feel horrible, even after repenting. This worldly sorrow is evil and leads to depression, discouragement, and death. Those who rub your nose in your sin, attempting to make you feel like dirt, (even after you have repented) are behaving like the devil. Satan is the accuser of the brethren, while Jesus is our Justifier and Savior.

As a child of God, you should feel bad when you sin, but that should all end when you repent and acknowledge your wrong. Why? Because it's over. God, Himself, has no memory of it, why should you? Feeling bad year after year yields death and destruction, not life and peace.

On the flip side, there are those who sin and feel absolutely terrible about it, yet they continue to do the behavior that is condemning them. I have witnessed ministers drunk as a skunk, crying over what they were doing, yet all the while continuing the action.

Jesus doesn't need you to feel bad about your sin; He needs you to quit choosing sin. Choose Him, His love for you, and His plan for your life. Jesus is not the one condemning you! He knows that all condemnation accomplishes is to reinforce the pattern of sin; it doesn't free you from sin. Don't believe me? Ask the children of Israel!

Jesus' love and kindness are what draws people to repentance. In our Scripture today, notice that

Jesus calls this woman's action what it was, sin! Yet it's not to make her feel bad. It was to let her know it was wrong and would destroy her if continued. He explicitly stated, "I am not condemning you." Even godly sorrow is not condemnation; it is a result of you acting like something you're not, therefore, it is against your nature.

You don't own a time machine. You cannot go back and undo what you did, but you can live for Jesus today!! Let the past go. If it is your present, repent and quit! Run to Jesus; He is not against you. He is for you! Allow Jesus to help you change what's on the outside to help reflect who you are on the inside.

Say this today:
Condemnation & worldly sorrow, I refuse you and command you to go in Jesus' Name! When I make mistakes, Jesus is not condemning me. He is loving me and empowering me to change! I choose righteousness over sin because that is who I am. I refuse to condemn myself or allow anyone else to condemn me over the sins of my past. Condemnation is not of God, it is the devil, and I will not have it in Jesus' Name.

YOU MESSED UP, BUT YOU ARE STILL HIS

Luke 15:20-21
"And he arose and came to his father. But when he was still a great way off, his father saw him and had compassion, and ran and fell on his neck and kissed him. And the son said to him, 'Father, I have sinned against heaven and in your sight, and am no longer worthy to be called your son.'"

Are you and your Heavenly Father focused on the same thing? If the answer to that question is, "No," then I'd recommend realigning your focus to His.

It would be good for you to read Luke 15:11-31. In this story, we see a son who has repented, yet wants to focus on his wrong action. He sees nothing but his sin and the destruction his choices caused. By doing so, he disqualifies himself from his father's love and very best.

On the other side of this, we see a father who is focusing on his son's change of heart, and his choice to leave sin and return home. He sees nothing but the overwhelming desire to love and bless his child.

This son is failing to see that, yes, he may have wrecked his life by his choices. But there was no choice he could make that would change his father's love for him.

The father understands that, yes, the son has messed up. But he is still his child. He loves him and is willing to help him! The father understands that no wrong action on the part of the son could keep him from loving his son.

What about your life? Isn't this just as true with you and your Heavenly Father? No matter what sin you commit, you cannot fall so far that His love for you won't reach you. If you want help and you want to change, your Father is focusing on the fact you came back, not that you left.

You will blow it. When you do, never give up. Your Father's love for you has not changed. He will help you!

Choose to focus on the fact you chose Jesus, not on the fact there was a day you didn't. Don't concentrate on what you did wrong yesterday; focus on your right decision today. You chose Jesus, and it's your Heavenly Father's best from here on out!!

Declare this today:
"In the Name of Jesus, I refuse to think about my past mistakes. Jesus, I choose to focus on you today! You are my Lord, not my past. You are running towards me to love me, not to condemn me. I am running toward you for help and love. You are mine, and I am yours. Thank you for giving me your very best right now today. Amen.

GOD DESIRES TO BE KIND TO YOU

Ephesians 2:7
"That in the ages to come He might show the exceeding riches of His grace in His kindness toward us in Christ Jesus."

Do you ever think about what God really, really, really wants to do in your life? Is your first thought, "He wants to love me and be kind to me!"? Do you see His Will for your life as an act of kindness toward you? Do you take time to see Him as kind? Do you see His every action and request toward you as an act of kindness?

God desires to show you His Grace by those acts of love and kindness! But, I have had some people tell me, "Yes, Kurt, throughout the ages to come, that's true, but not in this present world." Really? Who told you that?

Romans 5:2 says we stand, right now, this very minute, in His Grace through faith. Isaiah 54:10 tells us after Jesus came that the mountains would depart before our loving Father's Grace towards us would stop. John 1:17 says Grace and Truth came through Jesus.

Jesus has come!

His Grace has come!

His Kindness has come!

Right now, TODAY.

If you will cooperate, that is what He desires for you. God wants to be kind to you, now and forever. He loves you, and that's what people who are genuinely in love do. They are kind to the ones that they love. And God doesn't have love towards you; He IS love towards you.

When God speaks to you through His Word or His Spirit, whatever He is asking you will be the best thing for you. How do you know that? Because Jesus is in love with you, and He wants to show you the limitlessness of His Grace through His kindness towards you. All the days of your life!

Pray this today:

"Lord, what do you want me to do today? For the rest of my life, I want to know! Because I know whatever it is, it is based on your overwhelming desire to show me your Grace through your kindness. You only want what is best for me and would bring me the greatest fulfillment! I will never again fear your instruction or run when you speak. You want better for me than I do! And Lord, because I know you only want to be kind to me, whenever you make it clear to me what you are saying, I will obey without hesitation or question! I love you, Jesus!

ONE QUESTION: ARE YOU HIS?

2 Samuel 9:6
"Now when Mephibosheth the son of Jonathan, the son of Saul, had come to David, he fell on his face and prostrated himself. Then David said, 'Mephibosheth?' And he answered, 'Here is your servant!'"

In our last devotional, we talked about how God desires to be kind towards you; but, what does that look like exactly? Thankfully, we have an excellent example of this in 2 Samuel 9. (Before you continue reading this devotional, I'd encourage you to read the entire chapter.)

This chapter reveals the story of King David and Mephibosheth, the son of Jonathan, the Prince. King David and Jonathan made a covenant together out of the love and respect they shared for one another.

After David becomes King and Jonathan dies, David states that he desires to show the kindness of God to the children of Jonathan. By the very nature that he describes his actions as showing "the kindness of God," we can expect that what he does next is the type of behavior we can expect from God Himself.

David is the most powerful world leader in that day, and no one can make him do anything. What you see next is an act of love and choice. David begins to search out the child of Jonathan so he can show him the kindness of God. He spares no expense in searching for him and once found fully restores everything his father's family had lost. That is an amazing gift in itself, but David doesn't stop there. Next, he makes sure Mephibosheth has all the help he needs to work his newly gifted land. As if that was not enough, David tells him he won't have to touch any of the money David just gave him! From then on, Mephibosheth will dwell in the palace of the King, where David will take care of him and his family directly from his royal treasury. He is treated as one of King David's sons!

No one made David do this; he wanted to do it. He did whatever was needed to get Mephibosheth to the throne room to pour kindness and love upon him. David says he learned how to act this way from God. This was the kindness of God in action.

All Mephibosheth had to do to qualify for this kindness of God was to answer one question: "Are you Jonathan's son?" Or, to put it more directly, "Are you His?"

That was all David wanted to know. He did not want to know Mephibosheth's history and whether or not he was good, bad, or spoke against King David. Mephibosheth's behavior was not going to determine David's actions. The only qualification on the table was, "Are you His?" Because of this, the kindness of David's actions belonged to Mephibosheth. Not because he earned it, but because he was Jonathan's son.

Our Father God has only one question for you to qualify you for His kindness, "Do you belong to Jesus? Are you His?"

Your Heavenly Father has spared no expense to usher you into His throne room to pour out His kindness towards you. The authority and resources your granddaddy Adam threw away has been restored to you in Jesus. He then gave you His Holy Spirit to help you manage all of the great blessings He has poured out. Now He is telling you from this day forward, "You are my child and belong here with me!"

And how do you qualify for such lavish gifts?

Answer one question, and it's all yours…

Do you belong to Jesus? Are you His?

If the answer is yes, then all the resources of Heaven are yours!!

If you have never accepted Jesus as your Lord and Savior, won't you do it today? God The Father wants you as His very own child. He wants to pour His kindness on you!

If you have never accepted Jesus, pray this out loud right now:

"Father, I accept the price that Jesus paid for me. I believe that He was crucified for my sins and was raised from the dead for my justification. Right now, I declare that Jesus is my Lord. I am now God's child!"

If you are a child of God, say this:
"Father, I belong to Jesus. I am yours. I thank you that this is not a "me" story, so I will stop looking at myself and what I have done. I will now look to Jesus and what He has done for me because this

is a "Jesus" story. I receive your kindness towards me, and I qualify for it because I belong to Jesus. Thank you for the manifestation of your kindness towards me in every area of my life! I belong to you through my Lord Jesus, the One who did it all for me!"

DAY 31

STILL HAVING TROUBLE BELIEVING GOD'S LOVE? YOU ARE NOT ALONE

Romans 8:38-39
"For I am persuaded, that neither death nor life, nor angels nor principalities nor powers, nor things present nor things to come, nor height nor depth, nor any other created thing, shall be able to separate us from the love of God which is in Christ Jesus our Lord."

If some of the things we have talked about regarding the Love of God is hard for you to believe, you are not alone. Upon first exposure to these Truths, Paul did not believe them either.

He says here he had to be "persuaded" that nothing that currently exists or will exist can separate him from God's Love.

So, if you are still working on being "persuaded," rejoice! You are in good company because Paul was that way upon first hearing this, too. But Paul stayed with this Truth. We hope you stay with it, also!

Honestly, I was not persuaded the first time I saw the Love of God either. In some cases, it took me years to get through wrong thinking, self-loathing and a mistrust of what I was hearing from the Spirit of God. It was a tough barrier to break through as the thought of, "How could He possibly love someone like me?" plagued my mind. Even now, I still sometimes wonder how this is possible. But it doesn't change the fact that He does. He is Love! And He loves YOU, and He loves ME!

Even though I know this now, I realize that whatever I think I know of God's limitless love for you and me, it is far more than my human, natural reason can fathom.

However, I have spent years reading Scriptures on the Love of God over and over, rolling them over in my mind for countless hours. I no longer just know about the love of God, I believe and trust in His love for me. But it took me a long time to be persuaded! And now, I am so grateful I invested the time and stayed the course. Knowing AND Believing His love for me has changed my life.

This Truth will change your life, too! It is worth whatever time and effort it takes to become fully persuaded that Jesus is completely, head over heels in love with you! You can get there if you don't quit.

Even when you do get there, you will find it is far beyond anything you can see from where you are. After all, He is going to spend eternity showing us how much He loves us.

Pray this today from Ephesians 3:14-21:
"Father, for this reason, I bow my knees to you the Father of my Lord Jesus Christ, from whom the whole family in heaven and earth, including me, is named. I ask you, Father, to grant me, according to the riches of your glory, to be strengthened with might through your Spirit in my inner man, that Christ may dwell in my heart through faith; that I, being rooted and grounded in love, may be able to comprehend with all the saints, what is the width and length and depth and height— reveal to me the love of Christ which passes knowledge; that I may be filled with all the fullness of God. Now to you, who is able to do exceedingly abundantly above all that I ask or think, according to your power that works in me, (I make a choice to give free course to Your power and love!) be the glory

in my life by Christ Jesus to all generations, forever and ever. Amen."

ABOUT THE AUTHOR

Kurt Owen travels all around the world, teaching the uncompromised victory that Jesus brings for those willing to put their trust in Him. The hallmark of Kurt Owen Ministries message is one of victory through an intimate relationship with Jesus and the Word Of God taught in very practical, day-to-day "how-to" steps. Kurt never ceases to proclaim the message that because Jesus has risen, our victory is assured!

Kurt & his lovely wife, Terry, reside in Port Saint Lucie, Florida.

Made in the USA
Columbia, SC
29 November 2023

26830985R00081